Kid Power Tactics for Dealing with Depression

by Nicholas & Susan E. Dubuque

The Center for Applied Psychology, Inc.
King of Prussia, Pennsylvania

Kid Power Tactics for Dealing with Depression

by Nicholas & Susan E. Dubuque

Published by:
The Center for Applied Psychology, Inc.
P.O. Box 61587, King of Prussia, PA 19406 U.S.A.
Tel. 1-800-962-1141

The Center for Applied Psychology, Inc. is the publisher of Childswork/Childsplay, a catalog of products for mental health professionals, teachers, and parents who wish to help children with their social and emotional growth.

ISBN 1-882732-48-0

Dedication

This book is dedicated to the six million kids who are dealing with depression.

Acknowledgment

A great big thank you to Livia Jansen, Ph.D., for serving as our clinical advisor. Dr. Jansen offered many excellent suggestions regarding the contents of this book.

Contents

Introduction

"What do you want from me? I don't want to go out and play with the other kids. They're all dweebs. Besides, they don't want to play with me anyway. They all hate me!"

"School's a drag. My teachers are a drag. Life sucks."

"Sometimes it's like everything is closing in on me. Once I crawled out the window to get away."

"There are days when I feel OK. But sometimes all I want to do is crawl back in bed and sleep for a long time. I mean a really long time."

"I hate when she asks me, 'How was your day?' 'What did you learn?' It's like she's grilling me. And I just want to be left alone for a while. It's too much, too soon. Go away."

When you read these lines you may wonder, "Who would say something like that? Nobody feels that way!"

But if you think, "Hey, sometimes I feel just like that," then welcome to the club. Only it's not a real club. At least not one that you would want to join. But it is a really big group.

The group I am talking about is kids who are depressed. And there are six million of us. Just to give you an idea of how many that is; if you put six million skateboards end-to-end, the chain would reach from New York to San Francisco–eight times!

My name is Nicholas, and I am 11 years old. When I was 10, I was a pretty unhappy kid. No, I was more than unhappy. I was miserable. Finally, a doctor figured out what was wrong. Depression. At first I thought it was really weird, and I didn't want anybody to know. But then I became sort of a "Kid Expert" on depression. And now I know it's nothing to be embarrassed about.

Depression is not feeling a little down, like when you get a crummy grade on your book report. Or even a lot down if something really bad happens, like your grandfather dies. That would make anyone feel awful. The depression I'm talking about, real depression, is the bunch of lousy feelings that just sneak up and stick with you—for no reason at all.

Kids can experience two kinds of depression—the sad kind and the mad kind.

Kids who have the sad kind of depression are sort of like "Turtles." They just want to crawl in their shells and hide.

The kids with the mad kind of depression are like "Dragons." On the inside, Dragons may feel the same as Turtles, but to the world they may seem angry and disagreeable—and sometimes even mean.

I'm a Dragon. At least most of the time. But sometimes I feel like a Turtle. That's how depression is. Some days I feel terrific, and other times I don't.

Depressed kids are not bad kids. They don't want to be Turtles or Dragons. They don't want to be sad or mad. They're no different from other kids. They just want to be happy and liked. They want to feel confident and in control.

And that's what this book is all about. It's written for kids, by a kid (with some help from my Mom). It will help you understand what depression is and what it isn't, and what causes depression. And, most important of all, what you can do about it. That's right, what you can do to help yourself.

What Is Depression?

Well, to start with, depression is real. You're not faking it. You're not a crybaby. You're not stupid or crazy. Depression is an illness. And it can affect how you feel, think, and act. Here are some of the ways it can make you feel:

- **Sad.** You may cry a lot or look really down in the dumps.

- **Afraid or insecure.** It may seem like the world isn't a safe place to be.

- **Inadequate.** You may feel like you can't do anything right.

- **Alone.** You may think no one likes you or wants to be your friend.

- **Bummed.** Life just isn't fun. You may not feel like playing, hanging out with your friends, or doing things that you used to really like to do.

Sometimes depression can make you feel bad physically, too.

- **Tired.** Depression can sap your energy. You may have a difficult time falling asleep, or you may want to sleep all the time.

- **Just plain yucky.** Maybe you have headaches or stomachaches, or you just don't feel well.

- **Eating problems.** You might not feel like eating at all, or you may want to eat everything in the refrigerator. Depression can really mess up your appetite.

It can even be hard to think when you're depressed.

- **Concentration.** You may have a tough time keeping your mind on your school work or finishing assignments.

Depression can also make you behave in ways that even you don't like.

- **Restlessness.** You may be fidgety and can't sit still.

• **Getting in trouble.** Sometimes kids who are depressed make bad choices about things like drugs and drinking, or skipping school and stealing.

If you suffer from depression, be on the lookout for these signs. But remember, depression is not an excuse for being rude or lazy. It doesn't mean you can blow off school or not try your best. It's not permission to do stupid things or break the law. But the better you understand your feelings, the better you will be able to control your actions.

What Causes Depression?

Depression is not like the flu. You can't point to a germ or virus and say, "Ah ha, there's the cause." There may be several reasons for your depression—and even the experts don't always agree which one is the most important.

- **Family ties.** Some studies show that depression runs in families. If you have a problem with depression, the chances are pretty good that your parents or grandparents did, too.

- **Mind and body.** There's a lot of research today that shows a physical cause for depression. Here's how it works. The brain uses different types of chemicals to control how we feel, think, and act. These chemicals are called neurotransmitters. Depression may be caused when the neurotransmitters that control our emotions get out of balance.

- **Thinking and feeling.** Some experts believe that the way that we think can affect the way that we feel. If you think you're no good or that your future is hopeless, it might make you feel depressed. (It sure would make me feel that way.)

- **The world around us.** Kids today have to deal with a lot of stresses. School is demanding. Families are breaking up. Drugs. Guns on the playground. Peer pressure. No wonder more and more kids are getting depressed. Growing up is no picnic.

What does all this mean? You're not depressed because you're weak or bad, or because of anything you did wrong. Depression is an illness that is probably caused by some combination of what you inherited from your family, your own physical make-up, the way you think, and the world you live in.

How is Depression Treated?

OK. We know depression is an illness, just like chickenpox or diabetes. And like other illnesses, depression can be treated. In fact, just about everybody who is depressed and gets treatment gets better.

You will probably start with a visit to your family doctor, who will give you a check-up to make sure that there isn't some other reason why you seem depressed. A whole bunch of medical problems—from a bump on the head to not getting enough vitamins—can make you look and feel like you're depressed.

You may also see some other doctors, who will give you some more tests. But don't worry. Most of the stuff they ask you to do is pretty easy. Like looking at pictures and telling what you see. Or closing your eyes and touching your nose with your finger.

Once your doctor is sure that your feelings are caused by depression, there are several kinds of treatment.

> • **Medication.** Your doctor may give you medications called antidepressants. Antidepressants are not "happy pills." They won't make all your problems go away. But they will balance the chemicals in your brain (remember, the ones called neurotransmitters) so that your emotions can get back on track. When you first start taking medication, it might make you feel weird. But this usually goes away in a few days. And don't be impatient. It takes about four to six weeks for the medication to start making you feel better. Just hang in there.

> • **Therapy.** You may also see a therapist—a psychiatrist, psychologist, social worker, or counselor. A therapist is someone who is trained to help you feel better emotionally. There are different kinds of therapy. Some therapy involves talking about how you feel and what you can do to help yourself be happier. Sometimes your therapist will have you draw pictures or play with games, toys, or puppets. You may see your therapist alone, with your family, or with a group of other kids just like yourself.

Use Your "Kid Power"

Your parents, doctors, and teachers all want to help you. But there are many things you can do to help yourself. All kids have choices. You can choose to sit around feeling sorry for yourself. Or you can take responsibility for your feelings and actions.

The next section of this book will give you lots of ideas how you can use your own **Kid Power** to make yourself feel happier, healthier, and stronger. Each **Kid Power Tactic** has two sections. First, I'll give you some information. Then I'll share some activities that you can do. Read through all the Tactics, choose one you like, and give it a try. Then try some more.

These are not magical solutions. And not every Tactic will be right for you. But I'm sure you'll find a few ideas to help you feel more confident and in control when it comes to dealing with depression.

The time to take charge is now. It's all up to you.

Tactic #1

Take Your Medication.

If you have a headache, you take aspirin. If you have diabetes, you take insulin. If you have depression, you may take antidepressants. The first few days I took my medication, I felt like a zombie. Then after a few weeks, I started noticing some changes. I wasn't so angry all the time. It was a little easier to focus on my school work. Even my friends noticed I smiled and laughed more often.

Medication won't make your problems disappear. I think of my medication like a general in a war. The general can't win the battle all by him- or herself. It's his or her job to keep the soldiers in line so they can fight. That's how my medication is—it keeps me in order so I can make positive changes in my life.

I used to wonder if the other kids at school would laugh at me or think I was really a wacko because I take medication every day. Pretty soon I found out if I didn't make a big deal about it, they didn't either. Besides, I learned that lots of kids take medication for different reasons. Some take Ritalin because they have ADD—that stands for Attention Deficit Disorder. In other words, they have a hard time paying attention for very long. Other kids take medicine for asthma, allergies, and a bunch of other stuff.

Now Try This.

Visit your local drugstore and ask your pharmacist to explain how your medication works. What did you learn?

_____

_____

_____

How did you feel before you started taking medication?

_____

_____

_____

How do you feel when you take your medication?

_____

_____

_____

Tactic #2

Understand Your Feelings.

How are you feeling right now? Our feelings can change from day-to-day—sometimes faster than that—depending on who we're with, what we're doing, and what happens to us. Feelings aren't good or bad—they just are. But it's what you choose to do with those feelings that matters. The better you understand your feelings, the more you'll be able to control your actions. It's OK to feel angry, but it's not OK to break things or yell at people when you're mad.

Now Try This.

Here are just some of the feelings everyone has at one time or another. Think of a situation when you had each one of these feelings. What was happening at the time?

Happy

_____

_____

_____

Excited

_____

_____

_____

Sad

_____

_____

_____

Angry

_____

_____

_____

Embarrassed

_____

_____

_____

Afraid

_____

_____

_____

Surprised

_____

_____

_____

Guilty

_____

_____

_____

Jealous

_____

_____

_____

Proud

_____

_____

_____

Shy

_____

_____

_____

Hurt

_____

_____

_____

Sorry

_____

_____

_____

Tactic #3

Reach Out.

You've heard the telephone commercial "Reach out and touch someone." Well, the same thing works for kids, too. The next time you're feeling bored, lonely, or sad, here's what you can do. First, turn off the TV, put away all the video games, and get out of your room. Then make an effort to connect with another person.

Now Try This.

Here are a few ideas to try to really get in touch:

- Ask your mom or dad for a hug.

- Call your grandparents and tell them you love them.

- Share a feeling you've been keeping inside with someone you really trust—a parent, teacher, your therapist, a school counselor, or your best friend.

- Offer to help an elderly neighbor by taking out his trash or mowing her lawn. (Don't expect to be paid. Just do it to be nice.)

- Read a story to a little child.

- Do volunteer work for a local hospital or community group. The best way to forget about your own problems is to help someone else.

- Invite a friend to come over to your house, maybe someone you haven't seen for a while.

- Sort through all your old toys—you know, the things you don't play with anymore. And donate them to a local charity. Just think how happy you will make some child who doesn't have very much.

• Help out at the animal shelter. Dogs and cats need love and attention, too.

• Join a club like 4-H, Scouts, or a church group.

What are three things you can do the next time you feel bored, lonely or sad?

1.

2.

3.

Tactic #4

Make the Most of Therapy.

At first, I was mad at my mom and dad for making me go to therapy. None of my friends had to see a therapist every week. I was so embarrassed. I decided that they can make me go, but they can't make me talk. For weeks I just sat there and wouldn't say a word. Boy, was I dumb. The only one I was hurting was myself.

After a while I decided that if I didn't want to go to therapy forever, I'd better get to work. I also realized that my therapist isn't a mindreader. He can't help me if he doesn't know how I am feeling. You know what I discovered? When I started to open up and share things with my therapist, I felt better. I guess I'm not so dumb after all.

Now Try This.

What is one thing you would like to share with your therapist during your next visit?

_____

_____

_____

Set a goal for therapy. What would you like to accomplish? Maybe you want to stop arguing with your parents. Or make friends. You decide, and then share your goal with your therapist.

My goal is:

_____

_____

_____

Tactic #5

Express Yourself.

It's hard for some kids to put their feelings into words. Maybe you don't know what to say. Or maybe you think your parents or friends will laugh and think you're weird. You can still express your emotions in other ways.

Now Try This.

For one week, try expressing your feelings without words. Here are some ways to let other people know how you're feeling, without saying a thing.

- **Door hanger.** Choose different colors of paper to represent different feelings. You could use:

    Yellow for happy
    Red for mad
    Blue for sad
    Green for jealous
    Purple for afraid
    White for bored

Be sure to tell your parents what feeling each color stands for. Hang the colored paper that shows how you're feeling on your bedroom door. Tape it to the door or use string to hang it on the doorknob. When your family sees the colored paper, they'll know how you feel.

- **Plate mask.** Make Feelings Masks by drawing different expressions on paper plates —happy, sad, angry, hurt. Use a popsicle stick to make a handle. You can share your feelings by holding one of the masks in front of your face.

• **Stickers.** Draw faces that show different feelings on stickers—you can buy blank stickers at an office supply store. Wear the sticker that best shows how you're feeling that day.

• **Poster.** Make a Feelings Poster by drawing faces that show different feelings. Hang your poster on the refrigerator with magnets. You can place a little magnet next to the face that shows how you are feeling that day.

Does it help when others understand how you feel? How?

_____

_____

_____

Tactic #6

Keep a Journal.

Maybe you're not ready to tell other people how you feel. But remember, the feelings will still be there, and they want to come out. How about writing in a journal? It only takes a few minutes a day.

If you want to share something with your parents, your therapist, or a friend, you can show them what you wrote in your journal. But you don't have to show it to anyone. Ask your family to respect your privacy and not read your journal unless you say it's OK. And if that doesn't work—if your sister keeps sneaking a look—hide it in a secret place.

Now Try This.

Write in your journal every day for two weeks. If you can't think of anything to write, here are some ideas to help you get started:

- How did you feel today?
- What made you happy or sad?
- How did you handle your anger?
- What did you do today that made you feel proud?
- What would you like to do differently tomorrow?
- Who did you have a nice time with today?
- How did you solve a problem?
- What would you like to say to someone who made you feel sad or angry?

What have you learned about yourself by keeping a journal?

_____

_____

_____

Tactic #7

Tame the Dragon.

I'm a Dragon, and for me anger is one of the hardest emotions to control. Here are some ways that I discovered to help me deal with anger. Maybe they'll work for you, too.

Now Try This.

- Take a "chill break." When you start to feel angry and you don't want to get into an argument, take a five-minute break to chill out and cool down.

- Draw a picture of what your anger looks like. (Share it with your therapist if you want to.)

There are times when I feel angry inside for no reason at all. Here are some safe ways to get rid of your angry feelings:

- Punch a punching bag, a pillow, or a stuffed animal. Really beat it up until your arms get numb and tingly.

- Draw a picture of whatever it is that's bothering you and tear it up into little pieces.

- Make a clay model and really squish it.

- Throw a Nerf® ball at the wall or into your pillow.

- Bounce a ball really hard. (This one is definitely an outside activity—otherwise your mom or dad might be the angry one.)

The next time you deal with angry feelings, answer these questions:

What made you feel angry?

_____

_____

_____

How did you express your anger?

_____

_____

_____

What did you do "right?"

_____

_____

_____

What will you do differently the next time you feel angry?

_____

_____

_____

Tactic #8

You're in Control.

Sometimes my mom says I'm "impulsive." I hate that word. It means I have a hard time controlling myself. You know, like when I do something stupid, even though I know better, and then I feel sorry afterwards. Here's one way I discovered to help me stay in control. See if it works for you.

Now Try This.

Stop, Drop & Roll. Remember when you learned how to Stop, Drop & Roll in case your shirt or hair caught on fire? Well, when the fire is on the inside—like a fire-breathing Dragon—you can do the same thing. When you feel like you're about to lose control and do something you'll regret, try these three steps:

1. **Stop** - Stop whatever you're doing.

2. **Drop** - Sit down for a minute and count to 10.

3. **Roll** - Think about whatever it is that you're about to do. Let it roll around in your head for a little while.

The next time, before you act, stop and think about the consequences. Like when your mom tells you to turn off the TV and finish your homework, and you feel like yelling, "You can't make me!" Just stop and think. Is it worth losing TV for a week? You decide.

Tactic #9

Cut Your Losses.

Losing something that you care about can hurt a lot. It might be something big, like when a person you really love dies or your best friend moves away. Or maybe it's something not so big. But, if it's important to you, it's still a loss.

Now Try This.

- **Talk it out.** When you are really hurting inside, share your feelings. It's perfectly normal to be sad, angry, or afraid.

- **Holding on.** Sometimes it's good to hold onto your memories. When my Grandpa died, my mom gave me lots of his stuff—his army medals, high school class ring, pictures, and even the special flag from his funeral. I keep all of these things in a "memory box." Now, whenever I miss Grandpa, I look at my box and remember all the good times we had together.

- **Letting go.** When I didn't make the travel soccer team, I was pretty upset. I felt like something I wanted very badly was taken away from me. But sitting around feeling mad and sad didn't help. What did help was letting go. So, instead of being upset about soccer, I decided to learn a new sport—archery.

What have you lost that was important to you?

_____

_____

_____

What feelings did you have?

_____

_____

_____

How did you deal with this loss?

_____

_____

_____

Think of someone you miss, because they died, moved away, or you just don't see them very often. What did you like best or admire the most about this person?

_____

_____

_____

How can you be more like this special person?

_____

_____

_____

Tactic #10

Just Do It.

Exercise is terrific. When you exercise a lot your body releases chemicals—called endorphins—that really do make you feel better. It's kind of like a natural anti-depressant. It doesn't matter what you do—just do something that's good for your body and your emotions.

Now Try This.

Here are activities you can do with other people:

- Soccer
- Baseball
- Softball
- Basketball
- Tennis
- Football

But there are lots of fun things to do by yourself.

- Skateboarding
- Rollerblading
- Jogging
- Power walking
- Swimming
- Martial arts (Karate, Tae Kwon Do, Judo)
- Aerobics
- Weight lifting

Sometimes I like to do things that none of my other friends do. Everyone in school plays soccer. But I'm the only one in my class who shoots archery. It's really a lot of fun, and it makes me feel special, too.

Keep an exercise record. Each day write about the kind of exercise you did. Here's an example:

EXERCISE RECORD

DATE	ACTIVITY
9/25	Jogging with Mark - 1 1/2 miles
9/27	Rode bike - 3 miles
9/29	Soccer practice

When you get a really good workout, how does it make you feel?

_____

_____

_____

Tactic #11

Eat Right.

When you're down, you may not feel like eating, or you may want to eat all the time. Some kids who are depressed lose weight, and some gain it.

Have you ever heard the saying, "You are what you eat?" Well, it's true. Food is like fuel for your body. You can fill it up with junk or with "premium." So eat well-balanced meals. Fruits and vegetables will give you lots of vitamins. And breads, cereals, and pasta will give you energy.

Just don't pig out on sweets or greasy stuff—like candy, cookies, chips, hamburgers, french fries, and nachos. But you don't have to be a fanatic either. There is nothing wrong with having a Big Mac® or an ice cream cone once in a while.

Now Try This.

• **Next time you feel hungry, make a healthy choice.** Reach for something to eat that will really give you an energy boost like:

Fruit juice
Milk
An apple, orange, or banana
Raisins
Carrot or celery sticks
A cereal bar

• **Make a health shake for yourself.** And while you're at it, make one for a friend. Health shakes make a fast, nutritious breakfast. They're also great for those times when you just don't feel like eating, but you know you should. The recipe is simple:

1 cup of cold milk

1 banana or 1 cup of strawberries (or you can mix them together)

1 packet of instant hot chocolate mix (I use the sugar-free kind)

1/4 cup of egg substitute (My mom says that raw whole eggs can make you sick. Just the thought of eating a raw egg is enough to make me sick. But don't worry—you can't even taste it in the health shake.)

2 ice cubes

Put everything in the blender and mix it up. That's all there is to it.

TIP: Instead of using ice cubes, you can freeze the strawberries or bananas. Don't forget to peel the bananas before you freeze them, or they will turn black.

Tactic #12

Friends are Golden.

All kids want to be liked. But sometimes both Turtles and Dragons have problems making and keeping friends. Turtles are usually shy, and they may have a hard time talking to other kids and getting involved with activities. Dragons can be kind of prickly, and other kids may think they are angry or bossy or act like little kids.

Now Try This.

Here are some tips to help you make friends or to become a better friend to the ones you already have.

• Always treat your friends the way you want to be treated—follow the "Golden Rule."

• Think about your friends' feelings. People like to spend time with other people who make them feel good.

• People love to talk about themselves. The best way to start a conversation is to ask a question or make a comment about something the other person is interested in. Like:

That was a good book report you gave in class. Do you like reading about the Civil War?

I can't believe you made your dress. It's really neat.

Your dog is really well behaved. Did you train him?

Do you play any other sports besides softball?

I always do a belly flop. Could you show me how to do that dive?

• Don't always insist on doing what you want to do. Pick activities that you both like or take turns choosing what to do.

• Don't gossip or say things behind your friend's back.

• It is OK for you and your friend to have different opinions or like different things. The things that make each of us different are the things that make us special.

• Don't be jealous. If your friend does something special—like winning a race, being elected class president, or getting the lead in the school play—say "Congratulations!" and really mean it.

• Be honest and never lie to your friend.

• Listen when your friend is talking. You don't always have to have the last word.

• If you have a fight with your friend, make an effort to patch things up and don't hold a grudge.

Describe your ideal friend. What would this person be like?

_____

_____

_____

What do you like best about this person?

_____

_____

_____

How do you like to be treated by other people?

_____

_____

_____

What can you do to be a better friend?

_____

_____

_____

Tactic #13

Decode Other People's Feelings.

It's not only important to understand your own feelings. It's also important to be able to tell how other people are feeling, too. The more tuned-in you are to how your family and friends are feeling, the better you will be able to get along with them. And that will make everyone happier.

One way to tell how someone else is feeling is to look at the expression on his or her face. Other clues to watch for are:

- **Posture.** Is the person standing straight or all slumped over?
- **Eye contact.** Does the person look at you or down at the floor?
- **Speech.** Is the person talking fast or slow, loud or soft?

Now Try This.

Practice decoding by matching the list of feelings to the facial expressions.

Happy
Sad
Embarrassed
Proud
Excited
Angry
Sorry
Shy
Surprised
Confused
Jealous
Afraid

Tactic #14

Sleep Tight.

Depression can mess up your sleep. Sometimes my medication makes it hard for me to fall asleep at night. (That's called a side effect.)

Now Try This.

Here are some ways to help you if you have problems falling or staying asleep:

• Make sure you get plenty of exercise during the day, but not right before bed. That will just get you all wound up.

• Don't eat or drink anything with caffeine in the evening—like chocolate or cola drinks.

• Take a warm bath or shower.

• Play quietly in your room for a little while before bedtime.

• Read a book for a half-hour and then turn the lights out.

The next time you can't fall asleep, try this relaxation exercise:

1. Take three slow, deep breaths.

2. Starting with your feet, make your muscles very tight and then relax them. Tighten them again, and relax. Work all the way up your body, tightening and then relaxing the muscles in your legs, hands, arms, shoulders, neck, and face. Do this very slowly, one group of muscles at a time.

3. Picture yourself on the beach. You're lying on the soft sand. The sun feels warm on your face. Imagine that you're listening to the waves hitting the shore.

I'm starting to fall asleep just thinking about it. . . *ZZZZ*

Tactic #15

Become an Expert.

The more you learn about depression, the more in control you will feel. Why don't you become a "Kid Expert" too?

Now Try This.

You can start by reading books to help you handle any problems you may have, like dealing with anger, feeling good about yourself, making friends, or going to therapy. Here are some of my favorites:

The Best Friends Book
Sharon McCoy and Sheryl Scarborough

Making Friends
Kate Petty and Charlotte Firmin

Sharing
Debbie Pincus

I Was So Mad!
Norma Simon

When Emily Woke Up Angry
Riana Duncan

Everything I Do You Blame on Me!: A Book to Help Children Control Their Anger
Allyson Aborn, M.S.W., C.S.W.

The Very Angry Day That Amy Didn't Have
Lawrence E. Shapiro, Ph.D.

Stick Up for Yourself! Every Kid's Guide to Personal Power and Positive Self-Esteem
Gershen Kaufman, Ph.D. and Lev Raphael, Ph.D.

Don't Feed the Monster on Tuesday!: The Children's Self-Esteem Book
Adolph Moser, Ed.D.

Let's Learn About Magnificent Me
Jeri A. Carroll

Feeling Good About Yourself
Debbie Pincus

When Mom and Dad Separate: Children Can Learn to Cope with Grief from Divorce
Marge Haegaard

When Your Parents Get A Divorce: A Kid's Journal
Ann Banks

A Boys' and Girls' Book About Divorce
Richard A. Gardner, M.D.

Sometimes I Drive My Mom Crazy, But I Know She's Crazy About Me: A Self-Esteem Book for ADHD Children
Lawrence E. Shapiro, Ph.D.

Double-Dip Feelings: Stories to Help Children Understand Emotions
Barbara S. Cain, M.S.W.

Don't Pop Your Cork on Mondays!: The Children's Anti-Stress Book
Adolph Moser, Ed.D.

Take A Deep Breath: The Kid's Play-Away Stress Book
Laura Slap-Shelton, Psy.D. and Lawrence E. Shapiro, Ph.D.

A Child's First Book About Play Therapy
Marc A. Nemirott, Ph.D.

Read one book from the list. Or find one that you like at the library. What did you learn that will help you?

_____

_____

_____

Interview your family doctor or therapist. Here are some questions you can ask:

- What do you think causes depression?
- Do you treat a lot of kids with depression?
- What do other kids do to help themselves feel better?

Write a school paper or do a project on depression.

Call the National Mental Health Association and ask to be sent brochures on depression. The number is 1-800-969-6642. It's a toll-free number, but be sure it's OK with your parents before you call.

Ask your parents, therapist, or family doctor about joining a support group. Support groups are made up of other kids with depression. It's a great way to share feelings and ideas.

Stay in Touch.

I'd be lying if I said depression was a good thing. But it's not the end of the world. Depression is not a mystery—it's an illness that affects more than six million kids, just like me. And maybe just like you.

I hope this book has helped you understand more about depression—what it is, what causes it, and how it can be treated. And I hope you've learned some ways to help yourself. Most of all, I hope you realize that you're not to blame, and you're not alone.

If you'd like to connect with someone who will really understand, please write to me. I'd like to hear about your ups and your downs. Maybe you have a Kid Power Tactic of your own to share. Here's my address:

Nicholas Dubuque
11232 Midlothian Turnpike
P.O. Box 124
Richmond, VA 23235

Maybe we can work together—combining our Kid Power—to tame the Dragon and bring out the Turtle in each of us.

Now that you're a 'kid expert,' you can help your mom or dad learn about depression, too. Ask them to read *A Parent's Survival Guide to Childhood Depression*. It explains all about depression, what causes it and how its treated. It gives lots of tips for parents who want to help their kids deal with depression. (And it must be good, 'cause my mom wrote it!)

A Parent's Survival Guide to Childhood Depression is published by The Center for Applied Psychology, Inc., King of Prussia, PA., and can be ordered by calling 1-800-962-1141.

About the Authors

Susan E. Dubuque combines being a mom—including coaching her son's soccer team—with an active, demanding career. In her position as president of MSI, a marketing and advertising firm, she travels extensively and is a frequent lecturer on topics ranging from successful marketing strategies to personality profiling.

Ms. Dubuque has a B.A. in Psychology and an M.Ed. in Counseling.

Nicholas Dubuque is a sixth grade student at Richmond Montessori School. In his spare time he enjoys soccer, archery, Tae Kwon Do and collecting Civil War relics.

The Dubuques live in Richmond, Virginia.